Canine Cappuccino

MORE MUSINGS

Jennifer Perry

Canine Cappuccino by Jennifer Perry
Published by Dexter Press

Copyright © 2013 by Jennifer Perry
www.jenniferperry-author.com

Author services provided by Pedernales Publishing, LLC
www.pedernalespublishing.com

Cover Art by Barbara Rainess, Pedernales Publishing, LLC.

All rights reserved. No part of this book may be used or reproduced in any form by any electronic or mechanical means (including photocopying, recording, or information storage and retrieval) whatsoever without permission in writing from the author, except in the case of brief quotations embodied in critical articles and reviews.

Library of Congress Control Number: 2013949332

ISBN 978-0-9899207-0-4 Paperback Edition
ISBN 978-0-9899207-1-1 Digital Edition

Printed in the United States of America

Acknowledgements

Writing is, at its core, a solitary endeavor. And yet nobody can do it alone.

Or if they do, no one will ever know about it.

Taking my odd and occasionally demented musings and turning them into something that can be offered to the world and (hopefully) sold, truly takes a village.

And I, the village idiot, would like to thank all those who helped:

Barbara and Jose from Pedernales Publishing, who looked at my improperly formatted initial submission and thought that, just maybe, there might be something there worth printing.

Dan Flannery, executive editor, and Larry Gallup, editor/opinion, at the Appleton (WI) Post-Crescent. Thanks for giving me the opportunity to be a Community Columnist and unleash 800 words (or slightly more) on the Fox Valley every ten weeks.

My friends, for their encouragement, inspiration, and support, and for enriching my life in countless ways. Special thanks to Jeanne for steering me toward Pedernales.

Mills, Matt, Andrew, and Becky. I am so happy and fortunate to have you as my family. I love you to Punta Cana and back (there's no way you'll get me to the moon). Endless thanks to Mills for his computer expertise, to Matt for helping with titles and the order of the chapters, to Andrew for moral support and for grilling the best birthday steaks ever, and to Becky for the Key Lime cupcakes and for inspiring the little boy across the street to tell his mom, "Hey, they finally got a girl over there!"

And finally, to Dexter, my doggie muse, who as of this writing is an elderly gentleman but remains as happy, as quirky, and as beloved as ever.

Jennifer Perry
August 2013

Contents

Acknowledgements   iii

TAKE THIS JOB AND...WRITE ABOUT IT   1

Pee, Little Pilgrim   7

Truth and Lifest   13

Occupy Indianapolis   23

"Is Bob There?"   31

I Said, "I DO!!!"   39

Shingle Bells and Whistles   47

Roofing, Writing, and an R-Word For Costuming   53

Dreams From My Grandfather   59

Love in the Time of Choler   65

HAPPY HOLIDAYS FROM THE BIXLERS!   73

Agenda Bender   79

Dexter and Harry and Bear...Oh My   85

A Pain in the...   91

LAND OF THE FURRY, HOME OF THE SHAVED   99

Pit Bulls#&!   105

All Rise   113

Twenty Murdered Children   121

Cranium Scrapings   129

One of the Big Kids   135

Bread and Family Circuses   141

After the Attack   147

RED HOT (flash) FANTASY   153

The Reports of My Twittering Have Been Greatly Exaggerated   161

Knots and Loose Ends   169

Canine Cappuccino

MORE MUSINGS

TAKE THIS JOB AND...WRITE ABOUT IT

s 2011 wound down, I decided, for various reasons, to seek new employment.

And that's how I found myself, on the first work day of this year, sitting in a training room with 12 other newbies, each of whom was young enough to be my child.

In fact, had I begun reproducing just a bit sooner, and had my offspring done the same, some of my new co-workers could be my grandchildren.

Not so long ago, I was almost always the youngest person in whichever group I found myself. These days, I am frequently the oldest.

This, in itself, is not a bad thing.

It's what happens when you don't die.

But in this case, I, who have always had difficulty with technology, was trying to learn the computer skills required for our new job alongside people who have used computers since their earliest days.

And to make matters worse, I had completely forgotten that one of the symptoms of menopause is memory impairment.

Fortunately for me, my young fellow trainees were all extremely kind and helpful to the addled old lady in their midst. No one looked down on me.

Well, they did, but only because I'm so short.

I should probably tell you what my new job entails. But on one of our first days of training I signed a non-disclosure clause, and those first few days were such a blur that I don't remember exactly what it was that I agreed to non-disclose.

I can tell you, I think, that I take inbound telephone calls. And prior to this job, I did have some familiarity with call centers because both my sons and several of their friends are customer service reps for a major cable company.

One of the interesting things about call centers, considering that the customers never see the CSRs, is that there is a dress code.

Generally this means business casual, except on Fridays and weekends, because apparently those callers can't tell, or don't care, what their CSRs are wearing.

And at the cable call center, business casual means either black or khaki pants with no extra pockets, because heaven forbid that Bertha Waggenfloss from Maumee, Ohio should call about her cable bill and say, "I don't understand this franchise fee, and...young man, are you wearing *cargo pants?*"

At my call center, I can purchase a jean-wearing day by donating a dollar to a featured charity. I can also earn a free jean day by having perfect attendance.

Perfect attendance doesn't mean simply showing up for work on the correct day at the proper time. It also involves adhering to a very specific break schedule. And this is actually harder than it sounds, because the coffee you drink at 7 AM doesn't necessarily feel like waiting until 10:45 to be dealt with.

In some ways it's like being back in kindergarten, but without the compulsory nap, which is too bad because most days I could really use one.

This is partially because I have had a lot of trouble sleeping lately (which I had also forgotten is a symptom of menopause). Whether from the stress of a new job, getting up very early, or having an elderly dog who asks to go outside at 4 AM, I have had a number of sleepless nights, the kind where your brain simply refuses to shut down and your nocturnal thoughts include, but are certainly not limited to, the negative health consequences of sleeplessness.

So I went to my doctor and got a prescription for Ambien™. Well, the generic equivalent, but still.

And then I discovered that for the prescription to do any good, you have to actually take the pills.

I was initially reluctant to do this because, while whether I am smarter than a fifth-grader is open to debate, I am roughly the size of one, and I have had bad reactions to medications in the past.

And Ambien™, like other sleep medications, has been known to cause sleepwalking, and other odd activities like sleep-cooking and sleep-driving.

I don't like to cook, and I have a hard time believing that my Sleeping Self would feel differently.

But I do like to drive, and so the night I finally took my first dose, I hid my car keys, hoping that Sleeping Self wouldn't find them and take my Jetta for a spin.

So far it's going well. I take half the adult dose, and I am very careful to heed the warning about not operating heavy machinery. And for me at least, once the sleeping pill kicks in, even the TV remote becomes heavy machinery.

I do miss my 22-year-old brain (I miss that body too, though at this point I would settle for the brain), but I would like to believe that what I have lost in mental acuity I can hopefully make up for with life experience.

And what I have learned is that when a situation is difficult, if you continue to show up, if you keep just putting one foot in front of the other, things can get better.

And they have. The computer programs that seemed so daunting make sense to me now, at least most of the time.

In a lovely bit of role reversal, both of my sons have told me that they are proud of me.

I am learning something every day, which I have heard is good for my aging brain.

Plus, it's Friday, so I get to wear jeans.

Pee, Little Pilgrim

The story you are about to read is true.

The names could have been changed, because I'm not sure that my friends "Tom" and "Mary" want you to know that this article is about "them" and their cat, "Pilgrim."

I should tell you that I am not a cat person, though I will say that the litter-box arrangement worked out by Pilgrim's feline forebears is vastly superior to the deal negotiated by the early canines, which states that, in exchange for food, shelter, and walkies, the dogs agree to take their business outside no matter how bad the weather might be.

My current canine, "Dexter," disputes this agreement whenever it rains and during all ten months of winter, shooting me looks that range from the relatively mild "I can't believe you're making me do this" to the far more disturbing "Tonight I plan to kill you in your sleep."

At which point I remind him that I didn't make the rules, and that a deal is a deal, and it's not my fault that his people didn't hold out for a better one.

But even a win-win situation like the litter box can go awry, and this is what happened with Pilgrim.

It wasn't that he was misfiring, as I have heard can happen. Rather, he wasn't firing at all, due to a chronic urinary blockage.

Each recurrence of this condition required a costly trip to the vet to get the poor little guy unplugged. By trip # 4 or so, Tom and Mary were beginning to think that this might be Pilgrim's last roundup.

But then the vet had an idea.

The plumbing problem could be permanently fixed, she said, by turning Pilgrim into a female.

If that's not enough to send all the men out there running for the Flomax™, I'm not sure what is.

As of this writing, there has been no Pilgrimage to Transgenderland. Tom and Mary opted instead for a medicinal cat food which, though frighteningly expensive, has kept things running smoothly.

In other medical news, my son "Matt" has regained full use of his right wrist after breaking it during a mosh-pit melee in February. And because he is a guy, he thinks that the Frankenstein scar that runs up the inside of his forearm is cool.

The scar is the result of the wrist having to be surgically re-broken and re-set after healing improperly.

The night before the surgery Matt came down with a virus, but even though he was sick, the doctor felt that time was of the essence, and because he wouldn't be under general anesthesia, they could proceed with the operation.

But the combination of fever and sedation can do strange things, and afterward, Matt had the lingering feeling that he might have said some bizarre things during the procedure.

So at his post-op checkup, when the doctor asked if we had any questions, Matt wanted to know if he had in fact said anything strange.

The doctor shifted uncomfortably in his chair. "Well…" he began, "you did go on a rant about people in Madison. And Iowa."

Matt vaguely remembered that, though he doesn't know why he was so upset with those people.

"Was there anything else?" he asked.

The doctor had a deer-in-the-headlights expression, and shifted again in his seat. "Well...you were really mad at your toes."

"My toes?" Matt asked. "Why was I mad at my toes?"

"I don't know, but you asked me to cut them off!"

(Fortunately he is an upper-extremity doctor, and he doesn't do toes.)

There was more. The doctor continued, "But before you asked me to cut off your toes, you named them all!"

Matt and I were laughing nearly uncontrollably by this time. And while the doctor is a very nice guy and a wonderful surgeon, I began to get the feeling that perhaps he prefers talking to other people when those people are sedated.

Still, he persevered.

"What were their names?" Matt wondered.

"Well, the only one I can remember is 'Little B@#$@&d.'"

We are still not sure if that's the only one he could remember, or the only one he felt he could repeat.

Either way, Matt and his toes seem to have come to an understanding.

And Pilgrim the cat, at last report, is still going with the flow.

Things are looking up.

Except that it's snowing again, it's really cold, and Dexter has been looking at me strangely all day.

Truth and Lifest

The Apocalypse occurred on Friday, July 9, 2010. Perhaps you missed it.

A little after 8 P.M. CDT on the cataclysmic day, 62-year-old author and theologian Jim Wallis walked onto the main stage as the keynote speaker at Lifest, a five-day Christian festival in Oshkosh, Wis.

A few people waited until he had been introduced before getting up and leaving. Most stayed and listened attentively. He spoke for about 35 minutes, after which singer Shaun Groves spoke on behalf of humanitarian organization Compassion International, and then the headline band, Newsboys, took the stage.

The third day of Lifest had come and gone. And God saw that it was good.

Bob Lenz, the founder and president of Life Promotions, which puts on Lifest, had invited Jim Wallis to speak because he has read his books and spent time with him and felt that his core message that "any gospel that isn't good news to the poor is not the gospel of Jesus Christ" was a timely and challenging one from which the people attending Lifest would benefit.

Six months ago, none of this would have been newsworthy. It probably wouldn't have even been column-worthy. Six months ago, most of the Lifest attendees knew very little about Jim Wallis. Most had never heard of him.

Then all hell broke loose. And by "all hell," I mean the biggest dispute over a definition since Bill Clinton had a problem with the word "is."

The definition in question concerns the term "social justice." For some, it is apparently a code name for socialism and the forced redistribution of wealth. For Jim Wallis, and many others, it means addressing problems such as poverty and suffering, including the Biblical mandate to care for "the least of these."

Bob was aware that there was disagreement, and that some people had concerns about how Wallis might approach the topic at Lifest. Every year a few people have a problem with a particular speaker or band, so that is expected. With thousands attending each day, it's inevitable.

In the LP office, everyone was hard at work on the hundreds of details that go into putting on a large festival. But like watching darkening clouds on a humid summer afternoon, we were becoming aware that something ominous was headed our way.

A pastor in Appleton sent a letter to area churches and radio stations in which he declared his strong opposition to having Jim Wallis speak at Lifest. He enclosed a 14-page tract written by a member of his congregation that contained quotes from Wallis, many removed from their proper context and some almost 40 years old. They also expressed their opposition to, among others, Tony Campolo, Bill Hybels, Rick Warren, Bono, Jimmy Carter, and the Catholic Church. (It's very likely that they have issues with your grandmother's Shih Tzu, although that hasn't been confirmed.) The point being, it's very difficult to have a meaningful dialogue with people who choose to define themselves in terms of what they oppose.

Our office began receiving calls, letters, and emails. Some expressed concern over having a "left-wing liberal" at Lifest but were civil in tone, sparking lively but respectful conversations. Others were...not as civil.

One woman emailed to share the link she had posted to her "upwards of 600 friends" on Facebook, detailing her outrage and our stupidity at inviting Wallis to speak. She concluded by saying that we could respond to her, but since there was nothing we could say to change her mind there really wasn't much point.

A few weeks later she sent another email, upset because she had not gotten a response.

Another emailer chastised us for failing to do our homework on the man he repeatedly referred to as Jim Willis. And it's true that we did not properly vet Jim Willis the animal rescuer or Jim Willis the deceased Australian botanist. On the other hand, neither of them had been invited to speak at Lifest.

The tone and vehemence of the correspondence varied. But the vocabulary stayed remarkably similar.

Marxist. Socialist. Communist. Deceiver. Wolf in sheep's clothing.

For every call and email that the office received, Bob was getting twice as many. He was coming under tremendous pressure to cancel Wallis' appearance. He sought counsel from many people representing various viewpoints. I was honored to have been one of those people.

At one point he asked me if perhaps, for the sake of unity, the best thing might be to cancel. My response was that giving in to what I saw as bullying and intimidation would not be true unity;

it would only give a veneer of unity that would be destroyed the next time he did something with which these people disagreed. I said something about these people trying to get their way by coercion, and how it must feel like their collective foot was on his throat.

He said he agreed with everything I had said, except that it didn't feel like a foot to the throat, it felt like a punch in the gut, and it made him incredibly sad. And he started to cry.

It is generally not a wise career move to make one's boss cry, but if you know Bob at all, you will recognize this as completely normal behavior. He wears his huge heart on his sleeve in good times and bad. When he becomes a grandfather in a few months, I am not entirely sure he will survive the experience.

It's a terrible thing to watch a good man endure slander and ridicule. At the same time, it's inspiring to see him show the grace and dignity that Bob displayed throughout the entire ordeal.

A third option was considered for a time, and

that was to have Wallis speak on a side stage and not as a keynote speaker on the main stage. There were reasonable people on both sides of the debate who thought this might work, but the hardliners were not appeased, and ultimately Bob decided that Jim Wallis would speak as planned, as one of more than 50 speakers with varying viewpoints and emphases.

The calls and emails increased in both volume and vitriol. One woman called to inquire as to whether the decision to keep Wallis had been made, and when I told her that it had, she went into a tirade about "Obama's gay agenda" and how she knows what "those people" are like because she worked for a doctor who performed gender-reassignment surgery. She concluded by saying she would pray for our darkened brains and then slammed down the phone.

I'm still not sure how we got from Jim Wallis to sex changes, but it was not a pleasant trip and I don't recommend it.

Wallis was upgraded from a mere deceiver to a demonic force. This led me to wonder how to address him if I got the chance to meet him. Would "Your Decadence" be considered over-the-top? (I finally settled on "Mr. Wallis.") When I did get to meet him, and told him that I was the one who had been answering many of the calls, he put his arm around me and said, "Well, bless your heart."

Media from around the state had begun reporting on the controversy. One commenter to an online article in the Milwaukee Journal-Sentinel stated that he was praying for "another Katrina" to hit the city of Oshkosh because Jim Wallis was being allowed to speak. The weather on July 9, in case you're wondering, was sunny and clear, about 80 degrees.

In my personal opinion, much of the animosity displayed toward Wallis stems from the fact that he is considered to be a spiritual advisor to President Obama. In the eyes of some, that alone is enough to make him the antichrist. Or at least the antichrist's spiritual advisor.

Political discourse in this country has degenerated into a series of vile and vicious attacks.

Some are undoubtedly heartfelt; some are ratings-driven. And yes, it flows from both sides of the aisle.

The freedom to have differing opinions, and to express them publicly, is a constitutionally-guaranteed right. Dissent is woven into the fabric of our national identity. This is a good thing.

Demonizing another person because you disagree with their political and/or religious views is not. It's wrong. It's uncharitable. It's counter-productive. And it's dangerous.

Even a child can see it.

The day before Jim Wallis came to speak at Lifest, his 11-year-old son Luke was watching the news and needed to ask his father a question.

"Dad, that place where you're going…do the people there have guns?"

So, thanks to some cable news personalities and a few surly sycophants, our beautiful state has become, in the eyes of one little boy, something other than the home of the Green Bay Packers, or even that faraway land where odd but essentially harmless people use cheese as a fashion accessory.

It has become the place where he fears that his father will be murdered.

Since these events transpired three years ago, I have moved on from working at Life Promotions. Lifest has not had a similar controversy since. A radio station that boycotted in 2010 now has a regular program devoted to calling out sin and error, not just in "the world" but in other Christian ministries that may believe the Bible literally, but in a slightly different way.

And *the least of these* are, as ever, waiting in the margins.

Occupy Indianapolis

Today is the long-awaited day when we gather with friends and family to watch the Geico™ State Farm™ Capital One™ Super Bowl™ presented by…um, excuse me for a moment.

All right, I have just been informed that despite the strong corporate presence surrounding (one could even say "occupying") Lucas Oil™ Stadium in balmy Indianapolis, the National Football League championship game is still simply called the Super Bowl™, a name coined in the 60's as a nod to a child's toy called the Super Ball™, which was a hot Christmas item in the Dark Ages™ before iPads™.

In those same olden days, the football landscape looked much different. For example, in the college game, there were a few major bowl games played on or close to Jan.1, a couple of lesser ones, and everyone else waited for next year, which was actually later this year, but you get the point.

Today, there are more than 30 postseason bowl games, and so little boys can grow up dreaming of playing in the Meineke™ Car Care Bowl, the Belk™ Bowl, or the San Diego County Credit Union™ Poinsettia Bowl, which also serves to highlight the deepening divide in America over how to pronounce the word "poinsettia."

This bowl bonanza came about as college football, without a Super Ball of its own, pondered how to go about choosing a national champion.

"Why not just have a playoff?" you might ask.

Well, as it turns out, some people have asked that very question.

Sadly, those people have never been heard from again.

What happened instead was the birth of the Bowl Championship Series™.

The BCS came about at the urging of the six powerhouse college football conferences, which are bigger and richer than everyone else and desperate to stay that way.

These include our very own Big Ten, which hasn't actually had ten member schools since 1990 when Penn State joined, and currently has twelve.

It should not be confused with the Big 12, which has ten schools, or the Pac-12, or Pacific 12, which was known as the Pac-10 until recently adding teams from the coastal states of Colorado and Utah.

In the alternate universe of college football, this all makes sense. And we haven't even gotten to the Big East, which is better known as a basketball conference but has the BCS minimum number of eight football-playing schools and recently ensured that, despite some defections, they will still have enough with the addition of Boise State and San Diego State beginning in 2013.

It came to pass in 1998 that there would be four BCS bowl games—Rose, Fiesta, Sugar, and Orange—and the national championship game would rotate each year between those four sites. Each of the six major conferences would automatically get their conference champion into one of the games, with the other two participants chosen from all the other at-large teams. Each year's national championship game would feature a matchup of the two top-ranked teams in the BCS standings.

Determining the BCS standings involves a complex combination of the USA Today Coaches Poll, the Harris Interactive Poll, various computer rankings, two Magic 8-Balls™ (in case one says "Ask again later") and a panel of Labradoodles.

One of the continuing arguments against a playoff system is the added pressure that an extra game and more travel would supposedly put on the student-athletes.

It remains to be seen what effect being shuttled cross-country during bad-weather months in search of that elusive automatic BCS bid will have on the student-athletes at Boise State, which isn't even in eastern Idaho, or the ones in San Diego, who were apparently not content to stay home and play for poinsettias.

This past season's Allstate™ BCS National Championship Game (That's right, beginning in 2007, they snuck in an extra game in addition to the four BCS bowl games) featured #1 LSU against #2 Alabama, the first time two teams from the same conference had met in the championship game.

In 2003, when current Alabama head coach Nick Saban held the same position at LSU, he addressed that year's championship game controversy by saying, "I don't think anyone will know who the legitimate national champion is until all three teams in consideration get the opportunity to play one another."

This year, Saban reportedly voted #3 Oklahoma State as the fourth-best team in the final Coaches Poll in an attempt to ensure that Oklahoma State wouldn't leapfrog over Alabama in the final BCS standings and thus get the chance to play LSU in the championship game.

Alabama played well in a dull game and won the Allstate™ trophy. How they, or for that matter LSU, would have fared against Oklahoma State, or Oregon, or even the geographically-challenged boys from Boise will forever remain a mystery.

Say what you want about the No Fun League, but it still clings to the egalitarian notion that any team can get to the Super Bowl™, and that a championship should be decided on the field by teams that have earned the right, on the field, to be there.

Bunch of hippies.

Author's note: Not long after this column ran, Boise State, in a moment of geographic lucidity, changed its mind about joining the Big East. And the Big East changed its mind about remaining a football conference after so many defections. But on a positive note, preparing this column to be included in the book gave the author much practice in learning how to make the trademark™ sign.

"Is Bob There?"

The voice was young and female, a little shaky.

It was a Wednesday morning in July, the first day of Lifest, the five-day festival put on by Life Promotions. Bob Lenz, LP's founder and main speaker, was already down at the festival grounds, along with all my co-workers. I was in the office to field all those frantic "I lost my ticket!" calls before shutting things down and joining them.

"He's not here," I said. "Is there something I can do for you?"

The silence lasted so long that I thought maybe she had hung up. Then, very quietly, she said, "Sometimes…I feel…like I want to die…"

Had she been calling about a lost ticket, I would have known how to help her. But I have no training in crisis management, and there was no one there to guide me.

Still, I had one coherent thought, which was that if one of my children had made such a call, I would have wanted the person on the other end of the line to take it very, very seriously.

So I told her that I would try to reach Bob, but in the meantime I was going to get her some help.

I started pawing through the telephone directory by my desk, looking for the number of a local suicide hotline. And then an ominous thought occurred:

Bob speaks to kids all over the country.

"Where are you calling from?" I asked.

"Pennsylvania."

Oh, God, now what? I did the only thing I could think of: I called 911, told them the situation, and asked if they could get me the emergency number for the town in Pennsylvania where the girl had said she was living.

And soon, remarkably soon, I was talking to a young EMT named Corey in eastern Pennsylvania.

By this time the voice had a name—Ashley—and she had given me her phone number, but she wouldn't tell me her last name or her address.

And there was another problem—the phone number she had given me had an Ohio area code.

Corey needed me to check with Ashley that she was really calling from Pennsylvania. (They were both very patient with me as I alternated putting one on hold to talk to the other.) Ashley had lived for a time in Ohio, but was in fact living in Pennsylvania. When I told this to Corey, I thought it would be a simple matter of tracking Ashley through her cell phone.

As it turns out, this is not nearly as easy as they make it seem on TV.

The only way to resolve this was to get Ashley and Corey speaking directly. I asked Ashley if she would promise to call Corey if I in turn promised to keep trying to reach Bob.

And we both kept our word, because Ashley called me the next day, a little bewildered that the police had shown up at her door.

Bob has kept in touch with her, as has another LP speaker, Tiffany Thompson. The last I heard, she was doing well and had started college.

So what makes a sad teenager in Pennsylvania reach out to a shaggy-haired youth speaker half a continent away?

Bob's message is not unique, but apparently his ability to communicate it is.

He is genuine and gentle. He's not slick, or polished, or flashy.

He wears jeans and sneakers and untucked shirts.

He is completely, utterly unpretentious.

He radiates kindness.

The person that kids see on their school auditorium stages is exactly the same person that I see whenever he's in the office, which is rarely, because he's usually on a school auditorium stage.

He's going to Alaska. In February.

On purpose.

Life Promotions is a faith-based organization, but Bob's public-school talks are about things like respect and the value of each person, and no constitutional amendments are harmed in the making of them. And kids respond because the message is delivered with humor and humility, and because it's true.

It's the same basic truth that author Michael Connelly uses as the philosophy of his fictional detective Harry Bosch:

Everyone counts, or no one counts.

And since I have you all here, I'm going to do something I rarely do and climb up on a soapbox. (I feel taller already.)

School administrators who think that all is well in their institutions because the test scores are decent and the teams are winning need to get their heads out of their nether regions and look around.

Every day, in every school in this country, there are kids who are being subjected to physical, emotional, and verbal abuse that wouldn't be tolerated for a minute in the adult workplace.

If you were coming to work every day knowing that you would be the target of mocking, bullying, and/or physical intimidation, you would make sure that something was done about it. But for some reason, vulnerable, insecure teenagers, many with less-than-ideal home lives, are supposed to just suck it up and deal.

Your halls are full of the walking wounded, and some of them may not survive.

Please, please pay attention to them.

Everyone counts, or no one counts.

I Said, "I DO!!!"

In the late spring of 1977, as the college year was winding down, I was preparing for finals, and also for my wedding.

I was sitting with friends in the cafeteria, taking a break, when we were joined by another friend, Marian Magee.

Marian sat down and immediately turned to me. "You know," she said, "you're getting married on Flag Day."

In fact, I had not known that. Marian was from L.A., so I'm not sure how she knew it, though I had no reason to doubt her. But having grown up elsewhere, in the Dark Ages before Google, I also had no reason, at that time, to think that it was a particularly big deal. So I said:

Okay.

Marian pressed on. "Well…they have a parade."

Okay.

"It's a pretty big parade."

Okay. So?

"It starts at the same time as your wedding, and it ends up right outside your church."

So, it turns out that the Flag Day parade in Appleton, WI is, indeed, a pretty big parade. It is actually believed to be the largest of its kind in the entire United States.

But it was too late, at that point, to change our plans, and I still had finals to worry about, so I tried to put it out of my mind.

The big day arrived, hot and humid as only June in Wisconsin can be. We had chosen the date specifically because we wanted as many of our college friends as possible to be there, and many of them were, dressed in grownup clothes and smiling as the ceremony commenced.

Songs were sung, solemn pronouncements were made, and things were going quite well when the first strains of marching band music became audible.

It soon became very, very loud, and then we all heard a booming voice from the loudspeaker proclaim:

"LADIES AND GENTLEMEN, SENATOR BILL PROXMIRE!!!!"

He hadn't even been on our guest list.

"YAAAAAYYYYY!!!" said the crowd, which was now right outside the door of the church.

It was at this point that Mills' feisty little New England grandmother jumped from her seat and began marching up the aisle toward the door, presumably headed outside to tell all those rude people to pipe down because her grandson was trying to get married.

There's no telling what might have happened had she been successful, because this was a woman who became a little unhinged if her sour cream coffee cake turned out badly.

Fortunately she was intercepted by two of our ushers, who gently herded her back to her seat, and then began closing the windows of the already-sweltering church in a valiant, but ultimately futile, attempt to drown out the noise.

The minister gamely kept on reading from 1 Corinthians 13, the "love chapter."

Love is patient, we heard that day. Love is kind. And I have never heard this particular translation before or since, but I swear to you that on June 11, 1977, this is what the people assembled at All Saints Episcopal Church heard the minister read:

"Love does not parade itself."

I'm sure that somewhere it is written that it is very bad form to begin laughing almost hysterically during one's own wedding vows. But I think the wedding guests understood, and the parade-goers probably would have too.

The parade had dispersed by the time the reception ended, and we headed out for our honeymoon in Door County, where it was cold and blustery as only June in Wisconsin can be.

A few years later I was in the bank when a familiar-looking figure, flanked by two serious men in dark suits, approached me and stuck out his hand.

"Hi!" he said. "Bill Proxmire."

I looked at him, with his Andy Rooney eyebrows and his politician's grin, and said the first thing that popped into my head, which is seldom a good idea.

"Well, hi! You were at my wedding!"

His smile flickered, his nostrils flared, and he glanced first at one and then the other of the somber suits, silently pleading with them to help him escape from the crazy constituent who thought he had been at her wedding.

On subsequent Flag Days (or more correctly, the Saturday before the actual day, June 14), our sons set up a lemonade stand for the thirsty parade-goers, and they always turned a nice little profit.

This year's parade falls on our anniversary, and we will most likely head up to Door County to revisit some of our favorite haunts. I look forward to this every year, Mills probably less so, but he tells me that he enjoys being with me when I'm doing something I enjoy, which I think is lovely, and probably one of the main reasons we're still humming along after 34 years.

For those of you with a big day upcoming, I hope it arrives with a cloudless sky and pretty flowers and lots of smiling people in beautiful clothes wishing you well.

But should something go awry, and it probably will, it's good to keep in mind that life is full of imperfect yet wonderful moments, and contentment lies in learning to embrace them—appreciating what's in front of you, anticipating what's coming next.

Not unlike a parade.

Shingle Bells and Whistles

The nice thing about needing a new roof is that everyone knows a roofer.

Of course, "needing" is a relative term, and there turned out to be considerable disagreement between the two people living under our original roof about the necessity of procuring a new one. (Dexter the dog lives here too, but he doesn't get a vote because he is too easily swayed by special interest groups, which in Dexter's case is anyone with food.)

And speaking of Dexter, it has been pointed out to me that while he makes regular appearances in my work, my husband Mills does not. In fact, after Mills gave a copy of my book *Dog Coffee* to his friend Jim while Jim was recovering from heart surgery, I received a very nice note from Jim in which he told me how much he enjoyed the book but also specifically asked for "more embarrassing stories about Mills."

In this story, Mills is the person who looked at the fist-sized water stain on the ceiling of our son Matt's room and decided that we needed a new roof.

I am the person who looked at the same stain and thought, Matt has moved out, so, really, what's the problem?

Because my feeling about spending huge sums of money is, if you can't eat it, wear it, drive it, take it for walks, or give it away, what's the point?

But ultimately, cooler and potentially wetter heads prevailed and the search for a roofer commenced.

The first company we called sent over a very nice and competent man who spent an hour looking over the roof and assured us that his estimate would not be the lowest.

And after he gave us the estimate, and then had to defibrillate us by saying that we could go with a slightly less awesome shingle and save $1000, he was quite correct.

My husband is a fine person and a wonderful computer analyst but he is not a savvy businessman, and he was ready to sign the contract until I shot him The Look, which stopped him in his tracks. (You're welcome, Jim.)

Surely, I thought, one of the big home improvement stores would give us a better deal. They laughed at the utter absurdity of the first estimate, which was a big relief…and then they came in with an estimate that was $1000 higher.

And it was about this time that we discovered that the worst thing about needing a new roof is that everyone knows a roofer.

Our friend Mike called to recommend a guy he

was doing some volunteer work with, an older fellow who had done roofing in the past.

The Old Roofer thought that he, and maybe his son, and perhaps another guy, could do the roof in about a week and a half. He didn't have insurance, but promised not to sue if he fell off the roof and broke his neck.

Our son Andrew thought that his friend Dan could do the job, but Dan's errant fist had recently broken Andrew's nose in a mosh pit, and even though it was completely unintentional, we just didn't want those fists on our roof. (Ironically, this is not the friend known as Danger Dan. No word on whether he does roofing.)

My boss Chuck, who has built houses for a living, gave me the number of his go-to roofer. But when the go-to guy came to do the estimate, he forgot to bring his ladder, which—and I am certainly no expert—seems like a fairly important piece of equipment for a roofer.

It may well be that Chuck's guy is a roofing Rain Man, a shingle savant. But he just didn't inspire the confidence needed to hand over multiple thousands of dollars.

Finally, we went old-school and began calling companies we found in the Yellow Pages.

One of them returned my call and said that he could be over that afternoon around 3:30.

"But would you be mad if I showed up a little early?" he asked.

"I will try to keep my rage in check," I told him. He laughed, and a roofing relationship was born.

In fact, he started to call and drop by so often that he began appearing in my dreams.

The Dream Roofer's references all raved about the great job his company did, and now he can use us as a reference too, because in a day and a half our roof became the final resting place for 36 squares of hickory-colored architectural shingles, which are vastly superior to the old three-tab kind even though I still can't tell the difference.

We won't be taking any vacations in the near future, and Mills' tired old Grand Am will have to make it through at least one more winter.

But at least we know a roofer.

Roofing, Writing, and an R-Word For Costuming

So I wrote an article that was published in the newspaper.

The article was about our frustrating but ultimately successful search for a roofer. After the article ran, I received emails from six people asking for my help with their own roofing quests.

I'm sure the implications of that, in this economy, are as astonishing to you as they were to me.

Six people are reading my articles!

I know, right? And these appear to be actual people, not related to me by blood or friendship, as opposed to the poor longsuffering souls who are and know they're going to be asked, "So what did you think?"

Each article is like one of my babies, and each comes forth in its own unique way.

With some, I can remember exactly where I was and what I was doing when a thought or phrase that hadn't existed before suddenly arrived, the kind that makes you go "Now where did THAT come from?"

With others, the fact that I had to wrestle with them for days or even weeks makes the final result all the more meaningful.

However it happens, they are all, in some way, special to me. I suspect that anyone who creates anything feels that way about the thing they've created.

And like our natural children, our hope is that when they are sent out into the world, they will be treated with kindness and respect and, perhaps, even loved.

My artistic offspring are created with words. My friend Micky uses a needle and thread.

This past summer Micky was hired by the Attic Theater in Appleton to create the costumes for their production of *A Funny Thing Happened on the Way to the Forum*. This isn't the first time she has been asked to do this sort of thing, and this is in addition to her regular schedule as a bridal seamstress.

Micky is very talented and has a difficult time saying "no." As a result, she tends to take on too much in too short a time, and those of us who love her begin to worry about her health and well-being.

Her husband John and I were beginning to think it might take an intervention to keep her from exploding from the pressure.

But then Micky asked for my help with the Attic show. Not as a seamstress, because…well, we'll get to that. But as someone to lean on for moral support. And so I got to witness firsthand a true artist in action.

Micky told me that she doesn't plan out any of the costumes in a concrete way that people can see; she creates the look of the costumes as they come to her. This made perfect sense to me, because that's exactly how I write. But she felt that perhaps this was making some of the Attic people a little nervous.

I've known Micky since college, so our friendship has spanned decades, centuries, and even millennia. I wasn't a great student, but I was always diligent (some would say anal) about getting my work done on time. I frequently had the dream where you show up to class for the final exam and realize you haven't studied for it, or the one in which you haven't started the term paper that's due that day. In fact, 30 years removed from academic life, I still occasionally have that dream.

But Micky took it to another level—she turned that dream into reality on a fairly consistent basis. She pulled more all-nighters in a semester than most people do in a lifetime. She seemed to thrive on the adrenaline of desperation.

So the Attic people may have had reason to be a little concerned.

But after being backstage in the chaotic world of live theater, and seeing my friend completely calm and capable in the midst of it, I now believe that, instead of an intervention, we need to do everything in our power to ensure that Micky will continue in her work even if it kills her, which it just might. ("At least I'll die happy," she says.)

The costumes were imaginative and well-made and the cast loved them. I didn't arrive on the scene until the dress rehearsals, and my only real job was to help some of the men safety-pin their costumes to the shirts they wore underneath. Sadly, even this seemingly simple task proved to be beyond my abilities, and most of the men surreptitiously asked Micky for help, or resorted to self-pinning.

The actors, in addition to being impeccably costumed, were the nicest and most cohesive group of thespians I have ever encountered. During a long scene in which only the main characters were onstage, a large group of captains and harem girls and eunuchs sat on the dressing room floor playing a spirited game of Apples to Apples™. They were friendly and good-natured (even the eunuchs), encouraging to one another, warm and welcoming even to a late-to-the-party, thoroughly inept costume pinner.

And they put on a really good show.

Actors act, costumers costume, and writers write about actors and costumers. All of us hope that our efforts, our babies, will be appreciated and, perhaps, even loved.

But we press on regardless, because we really couldn't stop even if we wanted to.

I suppose that even a well-shingled roof is a work of art to the person who hammers the nails.

And I hope all six of you are enjoying yours.

Dreams From My Grandfather

The car trips to visit my mother's family always included a stop at HoJo's for saltwater taffy, and a bitter backseat turf war between my brother and me.

My mother grew up on a dairy farm in southeastern Ohio, the seventh of ten children and the only one to leave her native state.

My brother and I grew up in southwestern Michigan, and it was always a little disconcerting to spend time with these people who looked like our mother but sounded so different.

But it was fun to see our cousins, especially the oldest boy, Jim, with whom I shared a love of baseball and who was, to my ten-year-old eyes, the most gorgeous creature who ever graced the planet.

My feisty little grandmother seemed to have shrunk with each visit, which does not bode well for me, and my tall, lanky grandfather appeared ever more solemn. My most indelible memory of him is watching him eating a piece of pie. It was almost painful to watch as he slowly brought the fork, gripped unsteadily in his right hand, to his mouth.

His hand wasn't crippled, and he hadn't suffered an accident or a stroke.

My grandfather was left-handed.

But he grew up in a time and place where decent people used their right hands for eating and writing and pretty much everything else, and a child who showed signs of doing otherwise was considered rebellious, disobedient, and possibly demon-possessed.

So my grandfather lived as a right-handed person who wrote awkwardly and ate clumsily and took solace in the field and in the barn, because cows don't care which is the dominant hand when they're being milked.

Today, forcing a person to be right-handed seems barbaric and absurd. It's hard to imagine what a strange and lopsided game baseball would be without southpaws, or what music might sound like had Paul McCartney been forbidden from playing guitar in the way that seemed natural to him. (On the other hand, we may never have been subjected to *Wings*, but that's a discussion for another time.)

These thoughts about my grandfather woke me up in the middle of the night. There's just no way of predicting when the creative process will strike, or where it will lead once it occurs.

This time it led me to think about how much more we know now about what causes left-handedness than was known 100 years ago, and how much more will be known about things like homosexuality 100 years from now.

But, like all people in all times, we have to do the best we can with what we have and what we know, and what I know is this:

The gay kids who spent time at our house wanted exactly what every other kid wanted—a safe place to hang out, and copious amounts of pizza and caffeinated soda.

They were loud and annoying and polite and hilarious and loud—just like every other kid.

One young man in particular spent so much time at our house that at some point we figured we might as well just keep him. During one of the times that he lived with us, Kyle told me that if someone asked him to list ten things about himself, depending on his mood, being gay might not even make the cut.

Like being tall, and brown-eyed, it's one aspect of who he is. It doesn't define him; it certainly doesn't demonize him.

I don't know what discoveries will have been made 100 years from now about the complex combinations that result in some people being gay. But I doubt very much that it will prove to be as simple as merely choosing a lifestyle.

I think that vegans choose a lifestyle.

Kyle is gay. My grandfather was left-handed.

And he functioned in a right-handed world, but he would have functioned more effectively, and certainly more happily, had he simply been allowed to be the person he was born to be.

Love in the Time of Choler

> "If you let a hypocrite stand between you and God, the hypocrite is closer to God than you are." Troy Collier

A friend of mine – let's call her "Kris" – likes to post diverse and obscure quotations on her Facebook wall as a means of facilitating thought and discussion.

A few months ago, the quote at the beginning of this column appeared on her wall, and I had an immediate, strongly negative reaction. At work that day, Kris and I had a spirited but friendly discussion about it, during which she remarked that "there's probably an article in there."

My first thought was that the idea that a person's relationship with their creator is dependent upon other people is a flawed and dangerous one. (Although how that relationship is expressed in the way one treats others is a different story – more on that momentarily.)

Then, of course, there's the 500-pound gorilla of hypocrisy, a charge that has frequently been leveled against people of faith who, despite their beliefs, remain human and therefore imperfect.

Hypocrisy is not the sole province of any particular religious or ethnic group. Whether out of fear, frustration, fatigue, or a hundred other reasons, each of us, at times, behaves in a manner that is inconsistent with our values and best intentions.

It's a human failing.

Still, there is something particularly disheartening about religious hypocrisy, when those who claim to be filled with the very spirit of a loving God display behavior that is anything but loving.

It may not be possible, in these angry and partisan days, to have deeply held beliefs that run counter to what the church refers to as "the world" and not be thought intolerant, at least by some.

But I have always felt, and still do, that the vast majority of people respect those with deeply held beliefs, even if they strongly disagree with them, as long as those stated beliefs are accompanied by behavior that reinforces rather than contradicts them.

Far too often, however, it seems that those who talk the most about grace are the least willing to extend it to others, and the ones who claim in the most strident voices to be filled with God's love suggest, by their words and actions, that they are full of something else entirely.

There is a strain of very conservative Christianity that exhibits a meanness, an almost fiendish delight in demonizing those with whom they disagree. One of the latest recipients of their wrath is Michigan pastor and author Rob Bell.

As Mary Tyler Moore's Laura Petrie used to say, "Oh, Rob!"

Mr. Bell recently wrote a book called *Love Wins*, a lively little work which, unlike many of its most vociferous detractors, I have actually read. It caused an Evangelical firestorm before it was even released because of a video trailer in which Mr. Bell discusses the eternal destination of one Mohandas K. Gandhi. As in, it's not a good idea for anyone to assume that they know for certain where Gandhi might currently be residing.

Rob Bell is an elegant writer and engaging storyteller who likes to ask questions without necessarily providing all the answers. But to even suggest the possibility that the Gospel might be bigger and better than many have been led to believe brought down upon him enough Evangelical ire to stoke the fires of – well, a very hot place for a very long time.

A man named Ray Comfort wrote a rebuttal entitled "Rob Bell's Bad News For Jews" in which he tries to make the argument that if there is no eternal punishment, then the Nazis who committed such horrible atrocities in WWII get a free pass, and the Jews who suffered so terribly will not be avenged. He ends with the sentence: "There is good news for Jews. There is a Hell. Justice wins."

The human heart craves justice – punishment for the guilty, recompense for the innocent. But Mr. Comfort seems not to notice (or hopes that you won't) that there is an enormous problem with his reasoning. Jews, by definition, do not accept Jesus as their Lord and savior. So, according to Mr. Comfort's theology, they will be in Hell, tormented for all eternity, right alongside the very ones who tormented them in life.

That's not good news. It isn't even bad news.

It's the worst news ever.

The Christmas before last, my husband gave me a copy of Mitch Albom's book *Have a Little Faith* in which Mitch tells of reconnecting with his childhood rabbi when the rabbi asks Mitch to give the eulogy at his funeral.

The rabbi didn't have a television show, he didn't use guilt and fear to manipulate people into sending him money, he didn't preach in a mega-synagogue.

He served God by tending his little flock as well as he could for as long as he could. He treated everyone, whatever their beliefs, with the decency and respect he felt they deserved as a fellow child of God.

The idea that this kind and noble soul is, now and forevermore, suffering conscious agony because he didn't say certain words or adhere to one particular belief is abhorrent.

The Bible says that the first and greatest commandment is to love God, and the second is like it – to love one another. It also says that love for God is shown in how one keeps His commandments, and that His commandment is to love one another. To love the other people He loves... which is everyone.

Whatever your religious beliefs (or not), that's a pretty good way to live. Extending to other imperfect, fallible humans the grace that you know that you need, and hope will be extended to you.

Recognizing, in all humility, that no one has all the answers, especially the ones who act as though they do.

Treating others they way you want to be treated.

When that happens, everybody wins.

HAPPY HOLIDAYS FROM THE BIXLERS!

Dear Family and Friends:

Well, another busy year has come and gone, and you know what that means—it's time for the most special holiday treat of all: the annual newsletter from the Bixler clan!

And of course, it just wouldn't be complete without the official Bixler family foto! (See enclosed.)

That's Stereo,17, holding the reins of the camel, with Vinegar,13, and Weathervane,7, sharing the hump. Isn't that a hoot? And yes, that's Peoria,15, holding our brand new bundle of joy, little Macheesemo! We spelled it that way on purpose because we're from Wisconsin! Haha!

Honestly, have you ever seen such a photogenic bunch? Well, except for poor little Weathervane, but we all have fingers crossed that she'll grow into those ears!

The year started swimmingly at *chez* Bixler as Bill took us all on our traditional Caribbean vacation. This year we went to Aruba, which Bill says used to be owned by the Dutch.

And the Dutch live in *Holland* and also in *The Netherlands*, so that's like TWO MORE countries we visited!

On the home front, Bill's business has been going like gangbusters! (What recession?) In fact, this past year was so successful that Bill has been sent on a special assignment. Of course the children and I will miss him, but we'll visit as our schedules permit. He'll be gone for 3 ½ to 5 years, but we're told that with good behavior it could be less. Although knowing Bill, that's not likely! Haha!

For a while there it looked as though I might be going with him, but thank goodness the men in the dark suits believed me when I told them that I thought "The Pyramid Scheme" was a game show on NBC.

Handsome, athletic Stereo continues to excel in the classroom and on the gridiron, where he's won so many letters he could start his own alphabet! Ha! Of course, this past season was not an easy one, what with him having to wear that awful monitoring thingy on his ankle, which chafed terribly whenever he was tackled, and don't think the other players didn't know it!

And the teasing has been merciless. Honestly, you'd think he's the only high-spirited boy who ever pulled a harmless little prank!

And really, shouldn't the Pentagon's computers have better firewalls?

Anyhoo, once he's free to travel again he'll have his pick of colleges, and then the sky's the limit!

Peoria is a real go-getter, and so far has been able to keep up with her schoolwork and Twitter obligations while touring with her band to promote her new CD, "All the Different Sides of Love and Stuff." And if you'll allow me to indulge in a little maternal pride, it's pretty obvious that my little McIntosh didn't drop very far from the most exceptional tree in the orchard!!

Vinegar is soldiering on with her figure-skating career, even though at 13 she has developed what her big brother likes to call a little "junk in the trunk." Honestly, it's appalling how a little extra baggage in the caboose can wreak havoc on one's double Axel.

So I'm sad to report that we won't be heading to the Vancouver Olympics, but we've set our sights on 2014 even though Vinni will be a bit long in the tooth.

Weathervane is our little social butterfly, and even with everything else on my plate I'm quite happy to ferry her around to all her little play dates as long as she remembers to wear a hat.

You all know that it just isn't in me to complain, but even I will have to admit that taking care of a baby is not as easy as it once was, especially now that our beloved domestic, Consuela, has been forced to return to the Dominican Republic. Apparently, "drug-sniffing dog" is just not a phrase that translates well.

And by the by, did you know that the Dominican actually has to share its own island with a whole other country? Honestly, someone didn't plan THAT very well!

As most of you know, my run for Congress has had to be put on the back burner until things settle down a bit, but please keep sending in those contributions—legal appeals don't pay for themselves!!!

In spite of our trials and tribulations, I am looking forward to the coming year. And mum's the word, but there could be big doings around here soon. Can you say *reality show*?!!

Generic seasonal hugs and kisses,
Mistie

Agenda Bender

As nouns go, "agenda" has a fairly unremarkable history.

It comes from the Latin verb *agere* meaning "to do." It is defined as "a list, plan, outline, or the like, of things to be done or matters to be acted upon."

The only remotely controversial thing about it is that it is formally a plural, but we have come to think of it as a singular noun and have no problem slapping an "s" on the end of it when the mood strikes.

Here ends the grammar lesson. At some point we will still need to have a discussion about the current trend of nouning verbs and verbing nouns, but that will have to wait for another time, because today I have an...other topic in mind.

Despite its innocuous pedigree, it seems that lately the word *agenda* has begun to take on a vaguely malevolent, conspiratorial, almost sinister tone.

If you agree with someone's political or moral views, they are speaking the truth or standing up for what they believe. If you disagree with them politically, morally, or in any other way, they have an *agenda*.

The primary example of this—the Agenda-in-Chief—is the nefarious plot supposedly being implemented by our foreign-born, Hitleresque, business-hating, Communist, Muslim president.

The vitriol goes well beyond legitimate disagreement or concern about policy, and it doesn't seem to matter that many of the attributes ascribed to the president are untrue or at odds with each other.

But I suppose some amount of confusion is inevitable when you are talking about the Antichrist.

Another agenda was recently touched on by former Milwaukee Brewers pitcher Mark Knudson. In an op-ed for Mile High Sports about the possibility of having a gay teammate, Knudson wrote:

"Teamness is what fans demand from the teams they pay to watch. Any individual with an agenda that's even slightly different from that of the team hurts that cause."

I'm not sure why Mr. Knudson assumes that a gay player, while on the field of play, would want anything other than what his straight teammates want, which is presumably to play their best and work together to help the team win.

And that is what fans pay to watch—not what a particular player might be doing, or with whom, in his private life away from the field.

Plus, if a professional baseball player of any orientation is not concentrating fully on the task at hand during a game, he is one sharp line drive away from having his own off-field activities severely curtailed.

It's also possible, and even likely, that Mr. Knudson did share his locker room with a gay teammate—he simply didn't realize it.

After 50-plus years on this planet, I have learned that it is almost never a good idea to think about consenting adults with whom you interact—friends, neighbors, co-workers, or, God forbid, your own parents—engaged in sexual activity.

In fact, as I read over that last sentence, I think we can just go ahead and delete the word "almost."

It really is none of your business.

There are those who say that same-sex marriage, or even civil unions, would be the end of civilization as we know it. But no one ever really explains how traditional marriage would be imperiled, or why having more people in stable, loving, committed relationships would be a bad thing.

Some say that anything other than traditional marriage should be forbidden because of studies that suggest that children do best when raised in a home with both a mother and father present. And because the welfare of children should always be paramount, that is a valid point.

But it is not a guarantee of raising happy, well-adjusted adults, because no such guarantee exists. There is no magic formula.

For example, both of the Columbine killers came from intact, prosperous, traditional two-parent homes.

There are countless parents who begin rearing their children in a traditional setting, but then, for a number of reasons frequently beyond their control, eventually will be raising them alone.

When this occurs, other adults—relatives, friends, coaches, youth workers—can step in to help fill the void left by the absent parent (or the absent gender).

If this were not so, there would have been many fewer episodes of *Full House*.

When my son Matt was little, he told me that *Full House* was his idea of the perfect family.

"But," I wailed, "The mother is dead!"

He tried to explain that he liked the show simply because of its portrayal of a loving family all living together in a beautiful house.

"But the mother is dead!"

But I digress.

The gay people I know want to earn a decent living doing meaningful work. They want to travel, pursue hobbies, contribute in a positive way to their communities, and spend time with their loved ones. Some would like to get married.

Most people don't call that an agenda.

They call it being human.

Dexter and Harry and Bear...Oh My

There is a saying, my son tells me, that a skinny dog shames its master.

I am not ashamed.

Although maybe I should be, now that I know where Dexter has been going at night.

Dexter is almost ten now, an official doggie senior citizen, and very well fed. He's been around the block a few times, and he knows he has a good thing going here with us. His wandering days are over.

Or so I thought.

One night this past winter, the coldest night of the year, I let him out at bedtime, and 15 minutes later he still hadn't returned. I was bundling up to go out looking for him when he finally appeared at the door, looking very pleased with himself.

The next day I let him out prior to leaving for work, and I watched him saunter to the edge of our yard and disappear behind the neighbor's fence.

I followed him, and discovered what he had already found the night before—another kindly neighbor had left out pieces of bread for the hungry birds and rodents and, unwittingly, for one porcine pooch with entitlement issues.

My boys have a renewed appreciation for their little canine brother, and you can't really blame a dog for being a dog. But you can keep him from terrorizing the neighborhood, and so, for the time being at least, my little senior scofflaw is back on his tie-out lead.

It seems that quirky character dogs run in my family.

Many years ago, my uncle John spotted a beagle-like creature shivering by the side of the road and brought him home. The refugee, christened Harry, became a beloved family pet.

But Harry had one serious flaw as a beloved family pet—he was a leg-humper.

So, seeking more information, my aunt Beverly and my two young cousins took a trip to the library, where they encountered a stereotypical 1960's librarian named Olive.

My aunt explained the situation with Harry and asked if Olive could suggest a book that would help her young children understand their pet's behavior.

"I suggest," sniffed Olive, "that you get rid of the dog."

But they didn't, and Harry the Humper lived out

his days with his quirks, if not everything else, intact.

Once my family was dog-sitting, and Harry chased a squirrel up a tree, and by that I mean that he actually followed the squirrel up into the tree, and had gotten remarkably far before he remembered that dogs can't climb trees.

My father had to rescue him, employing a ladder and some words I wasn't normally allowed to hear.

My affinity for character dogs doesn't seem to help much with more traditional types, however.

My boss, youth speaker Bob Lenz, frequently travels with AJ the Illusionist and Bear, AJ's five-year-old Pomeranian mix.

Bear is obedient, well-trained, and highly intelligent. I have very little experience with that type of dog.

Even so, one day when Bear and AJ were in the

office and AJ needed to run some errands, I volunteered to be in charge of Bear.

Bear began his stay with me by visiting everyone's cubicle, which wasn't a problem in itself because everyone loves him. But even though he is a seasoned and conscientious performer, I was afraid that his essential dogness might lead him to find something disgusting to ingest, and I didn't want to have to explain to Bob and AJ why he was too ill to perform that night.

So I asked Bear to lie down by my desk while I did data entry. He complied, but it seems that, even with very obedient dogs, there is a statute of limitations on commands, and so every few minutes he would get up to wander, because it turns out that watching a human do data entry just isn't as fascinating to a dog as you might think.

Then I tried to engage him intellectually.

"Can you speak, Bear?" I asked.

"Arf!" said Bear. And then he cocked his head and stared at me, waiting for his reward.

The problem was, I hadn't actually been commanding Bear to speak; I was just making conversation. But clearly, Bear saw things differently, and was not at all amused at this egregious breach of protocol.

But I had no treat to give him, and so I turned back to my computer screen, hoping he would forget about me and wander off.

A few minutes later I turned to look, and he was still staring at me, burning his gaze into my wretched, treat-withholding soul.

It's probably best for everyone if I just stick to the quirky character dogs.

A Pain in the...

My doctor looked up from his computer and said, "It looks like you're overdue for both a mammogram AND a colonoscopy."

So I did what any reasonable person would do.

I offered to get two mammograms and skip the colonoscopy.

He was not amused. In fact, he fixed me with the kind of stare that doctors must surely reserve for otherwise-intelligent people who stubbornly refuse to get relatively easy, painless procedures that have been proven to save lives.

I had been dealing with this medical peer pressure for quite some time.

A few years ago, I was getting calls from a talking polyp whose name, if I remember correctly, was Pauly. It was part of a reverse-psychology campaign in which Pauly Polyp, in a thick New York accent, would beg me not to get a colonoscopy, for fear that his comfy abode in my large intestine would be discovered, and he would be forced to vacate the premises.

Thankfully, I lost the polyp when we dropped our landline. And since I now have a job in which I talk to people from Brooklyn and Long Island every day, I have come to suspect that he wasn't even a real New Yorker.

Besides, I had very rational and well-considered excuses—I mean reasons—for not getting a colonoscopy.

My grandmother lived to be 107 without ever having one. I have no family history of colon cancer. I was having no symptoms.

Canine Cappuccino

Plus, I really, really don't want to, and you can't make me. So there.

Then one day last spring, I woke up with mild discomfort in my abdomen. It wasn't troublesome, and it really only hurt if I pressed on it, which reminded me of the old joke:

PATIENT: Doc, it hurts when I do this.

DOCTOR: Then don't do that.

But it occurred to me that if the pain persisted and I had to go to the doctor, the first thing they would do is order a colonoscopy. So I called proactively to make the appointment.

And then, of course, the pain went away. But I decided to keep the appointment, if for no other reason than to get the medical professionals in my life off my case.

I already had the instructions that explained how to get ready for the procedure. They were very specific about what was involved—I needed to mix 64 oz. of G2 Gatorade™ (NOT regular

Gatorade) with one bottle, 238 grams, of polyethylene glycol.

Conspicuously absent from the instructions was any mention of why they want you to drink the devilish concoction, or what will begin to happen once you do.

And it is this part of the experience—the prep, also known as The Prep—that makes peaceful, well-intentioned people run away screaming.

It would be a much more popular event if you could go to, say, Taco Bell,™ let nature take its course, and then show up a few hours later as a walk-in, completely empty and ready for inspection.

But no.

I had opted for the one-day procedure, which meant I had to get up at 5 AM and begin The Prep immediately. I mixed the ingredients in a large pitcher, and then began to pour the contents into a coffee cup, so that I could pretend that I was merely sipping my morning brew, rather than sending weapons-grade liquid explosives on a search-and-destroy mission.

As I was sipping (8 ounces every 10-15 minutes), I looked through the instructions again, and saw this ominous line:

"If your prep doesn't work, repeat it."

I'm not sure at what point, after drinking 64 oz. of laxative-laced Gatorade™, you begin to suspect that things might not be going well—not moving along, as it were-and you need to risk going to the store for reinforcements.

Fortunately I didn't have to find out. Because for me—and here I will be as delicate as possible—the prep worked.

And worked. And worked.

And worked some more.

It worked while I was watching the news, and while I was doing the crossword.

It worked through several attempts at reading the same page of the same book.

At mid-morning it took a 15-minute break, giving me a ray of hope that, perhaps, the festivities were winding down.

And then it worked three times in five minutes.

As the unseen Mrs. Wolowitz said so memorably on *The Big Bang Theory*: "I'm like an upside-down volcano here!"

It was still working, a little, when it was time to go to the appointment.

Colonoscopy Fashion Tip: White pants are a no-no, even if it is after Memorial Day.

When you get to your appointment, you are given a pager to let you know when they are ready for you. Just like at Applebee's™, except that the table has wheels, and you are the entrée.

As for the procedure itself, you sleep right through it, which is probably best for everyone.

I had been told that it would be the best sleep I'd ever had, but I don't think that's true when you wake up, as I did, groggy and a little nauseated.

By the next morning, the nausea had passed. I had a headache that went away as soon as I had some coffee. I also had an unexpected visit from my dear old friend The Prep, which apparently (and very mistakenly) thought that I had missed its presence. And that was it.

So here is the part where I implore you, if you are age 50 or older, to do as I finally did, and not as I used to do. At worst, your colonoscopy might reveal a condition which, when caught early, is highly treatable.

And at best, you will have peace of mind, and ten years of freedom from the reproachful looks of your doctor.

Also, you shouldn't be getting any calls from talking polyps.

Although with election season upon us, I can't guarantee it.

LAND OF THE FURRY, HOME OF THE SHAVED

The mood in Rodentville, as the November elections approached, had become increasingly, relentlessly sour.

Late autumn is always a busy and bittersweet time in the yard, as the reality of winter's imminent arrival creates a heightened sense of urgency and, in some, an almost palpable anxiety.

Also, everyone starts putting on weight.

But this past November, and the months preceding it, had been more angry and contentious than anyone could remember.

Emblematic of how unpleasant things had become, no one could agree on why this had happened, when it had started, who was to blame, or what should be done to fix it.

Things had seemed so different just a few years earlier, when The Spaniel made history by becoming Rodentville's first canine mayor.

When he first arrived in the yard, with his striking speckled coat and his puppyish exuberance, everyone could tell that he would be going places. But no one could have predicted how rapid his ascent would be, or how soon it would begin.

His story was compelling. The son of a single mother, he and his lookalike brother were the only survivors from their litter of five. Taken from their overwhelmed mother, they were put into foster care and then adopted by different groups of two-leggers. Sadly, the brothers soon lost contact with each other.

The Spaniel quickly became a rising star in the Rodentville political scene. Not long after his arrival, he came upon a nest of baby bunnies.

Everyone watched in fascination, wondering what the young canine would do. He picked up one of the bunnies in his mouth and tenderly carried it into the house he shared with the two-leggers.

This won him the respect and admiration of the rabbit community, but undisguised scorn from many of the squirrels, who thought it showed that, should he become Mayor, he would be soft on matters of defense.

When he announced that he was running for Mayor, even some of his most ardent supporters worried that it might be too soon, for him and for Rodentville. Still, they eagerly supported his campaign, and he defeated his opponents—a bellicose badger, a grumpy groundhog, and a chatterbox of a chipmunk—in a near-landslide.

That a cocker spaniel, and a black-and-white one at that, had risen to the highest office in Rodentville filled many with an almost giddy sense of hope and optimism. It truly seemed as though anything might be possible.

"This is the most amazing thing to happen in my lifetime!" exulted a gray-whiskered rabbit. "I never thought I would live to see the day!"

Snarled an equally gray but much younger squirrel, "There they go again! Throwing their longer lifespans right in our faces!"

The situation The Spaniel faced was a daunting one. His election came in the middle of one of the bleakest times in Rodentville's history. Ongoing skirmishes with other yards, combined with a neighborhood-wide shortage of nuts and other resources, had many of the little denizens on the brink of despair.

The new mayor warned that tough times lay ahead, and that while things would get better, it wouldn't happen as quickly or as smoothly as everyone might want.

But some wondered if it would happen at all with such an inexperienced, untested leader. To them, the Spaniel was an arriviste, an elitist with an odd and scary-sounding name, a skillful howler with a resume as short as his docked tail.

This discontent was seized upon by the feathered pundits perched high above Rodentville on the telephone wire.

"I hope he fails!" squawked Thrush Limbaugh, as Glenn Beak and Bill O'Robin flapped their wings and bobbed their heads in agreement.

(They were frequently joined on the western end of the wire by Stephen T. Crowbert. But even though he seemed to say all the right things, he said them in such a way that some began to think that perhaps they were being mocked, and that Crowbert actually belonged on the other end of the wire, along with the likes of Jon Starling and Lewis Blackbird and Keith Oriolebermann, and even that random jay who wasn't really a part of either group, but liked to drop in from time to time.)

So as the November midterms approached, the shrieking and cawing had become so loud that no one was able to hear anyone else, even if they tried.

In an effort to help create a less-toxic environment, Jon Starling organized a gathering called the Flock to Forego Meanness, and it was extremely well-attended, even though some pretended not to notice ("Not see! Not see!" cried Glenn Beak).

The results of the November elections were unsurprising. The Mayor held onto his job, barely, but for the incumbent rodent representatives, it was a bloodbath. Everyone had an opinion on what it all meant, but, predictably, no one could agree on that either.

Then, just as torpor was beginning to set in, an amazing thing happened. Under the watchful eye of an elegant mallard with a pronounced limp who graciously agreed to delay his migration, the rodent representatives actually worked together to get some important legislation passed, offering a glimmer of hope for the future.

Because if there's anything to be learned in Rodentville, it's that different species will need to find ways to get along in order to benefit the yard they all love.

Pit Bulls#&!

On July 11, 2012, a condemned prisoner in Belfast, Northern Ireland was put to death.

He had languished on death row, lonely and frightened, for two years as appeals were filed and ultimately rejected. Pleas for clemency from social media, various petitions, and even the First Minister of Northern Ireland went unanswered.

All this occurred even though the condemned had committed no crime, much less been convicted of one.

Lennox the dog was "humanely put to sleep" because, in the opinion of the Belfast City Council, he too closely resembled a pit bull.

Pit bulls are an outlawed breed in the U.K. Lennox, a bulldog-Labrador mix, was taken from his home in 2010 after city officials measured his legs and snout and declared him to be "an illegal pit-bull terrier type."

The Belfast City Council declared Lennox to be "one of the most unpredictable and dangerous dogs" that its appointed expert had ever encountered, although the expert's examination and subsequent pronouncement were made after Lennox had been taken into custody, away from his familiar surroundings and the people he loved and trusted.

His owner, Caroline Barnes, acknowledged that Lennox could be somewhat aggressive with strangers, but testified that he had never bitten anyone, and that she kept him muzzled if there was a chance that he might become agitated.

Victoria Stilwell, the host of the Animal Planet

show *It's Me or the Dog*, offered to pay all the costs of rehoming Lennox in a country with less restrictive breed laws. Her offer was rejected.

Maybe the members of the Belfast City Council truly believed that they were protecting the public and doing the right thing.

More likely, it's a case of bureaucrats making a hasty, poorly-considered ruling and then refusing to reconsider or negotiate for fear of seeming weak or indecisive.

Or possibly, in a city that has seen so much horror and heartbreak, there simply wasn't enough compassion left for one insignificant family and their beloved pet.

This would probably be a good time to mention that my son and his fiancée have a rescued American Staffordshire terrier, a pit bull relative.

Sampson is gentle with the one-year-old boy who lives down the street. He begs for peanut butter and loves to be chased at the dog park.

He hides under the bed during thunderstorms.

He is, in every way, a wonderful companion.

Over the years, I have told a number of stories about another wonderful companion—my quirky cocker spaniel, Dexter.

One I haven't previously told involves a trip, several years ago, to a new groomer. Less than an hour after I dropped Dexter off, I got a call telling me I needed to pick him up right away.

When I arrived, Dexter was calm. He had been bathed but not yet shorn, so he was fluffy and very full-bodied, like a black-and-white Chia Pet™.

They told me that something—probably a vacuum, though we'll never really know—had set him off, and he had begun to snarl and snap at the groomer. He lost control of his bodily functions.

Fortunately, the groomers recognized that Dexter's behavior was an aberration, a one-time event completely out of character for such a gentle dog. He has never behaved like that before, or since.

But in that moment, my sweet little spaniel displayed more viciousness than many pit bulls ever do.

I'm not saying that city officials do not have the right, and the responsibility, to protect the public from dangerous animals and/or irresponsible owners.

They do, and they should.

But when that right is used unwisely or unfairly due to prejudice or fear or simple indifference, no one wins. We are not safer. We are merely poorer.

Zero tolerance policies, of which breed bans are just one example, are a politically expedient notion that can sound reassuringly tough while avoiding the inconvenience and effort of dealing with the nuances of individual cases.

There are those who say that people who care

deeply about animal welfare should spend more time caring about their fellow humans, as though the two were mutually exclusive.

They are not. Compassion for all, and especially for the weakest and most vulnerable among us, human and otherwise, should be welcomed and not criticized.

There are many problems in this world, but I think it's safe to say that too much empathy is not one of them.

Society benefits from every act of kindness, regardless of the recipient. Also, we would do well to remember that violence and cruelty toward animals has been shown to be a major red flag as a predictor of future crimes against humans.

And then there's this.

Here in Wisconsin, a man is accused of using his dog (initially, and incorrectly, identified as a pit bull) as a weapon against a young man he suspected of stealing from him.

He allegedly used the dog's leash to string the boy upside down—with help from the boy's own father—and then commanded the dog to attack him.

The question practically asks itself:

Which one is the real animal?

All Rise

As anyone who has watched a crime drama knows, everyone in this country has the right to an attorney.

It is not guaranteed, however, that everyone will have a good one.

And that is one of many observations from my new life as a juror.

During the summer I received a questionnaire from the county clerk's office regarding my suitability to serve on a jury. It seemed mainly concerned with establishing the fact that I live in Outagamie County, although it also wanted to make sure that I can understand English.

I filled it out, sent it in, and forgot about it until I received my official summons to report for jury duty on five specific days in September.

Friends began telling me of ways I could ensure that I wouldn't be picked for the actual jury. My son reminded me of Tina Fey's character on *30 Rock*, who showed up for court dressed as Princess Leia and told the judge she couldn't serve because she's a hologram.

But after years of watching *Law & Order*, I was curious about what the process was really like. I wanted to serve.

There was just one tiny, hopefully insignificant problem. The fourth of my five required days was the same day that Gordon Lightfoot was performing in Milwaukee.

It's possible to petition the court for a temporary hardship and be switched to a different month. But it was just one day, and I had been told that many cases settle prior to their trial dates, so I decided to fulfill my obligation and hope for the best.

The only thing I feared was that my first three days would all be cancelled, and I would have to show up as a newbie on the one day I truly didn't want to be there. But, really, what were the chances of that?

Well, as you've probably surmised, better than fair.

I called the jury message line the night before the fateful day, but unlike the previous three times, I was told to report the next morning at 8:45. (I was also advised to leave my cell phone, my pocket knife, and other "contraband of sorts" at home.)

What could I do? Could I even find a Princess Leia costume at that hour?

Eventually, of course, I did the only thing I could do—I showed up, still hoping for the best.

Perhaps, as I have heard often happens, the case had settled on the courthouse steps.

It hadn't.

Maybe I would know the judge, the defendant, or one of the attorneys.

I didn't.

Possibly I wouldn't be one of the first 20 potential jurors called into the jury box for voir dire.

I was.

So when the judge asked if any of us felt we could not be a fair and impartial juror, I did what I had sworn to do.

I told the truth.

I told him that, just for that day, I couldn't be fair and impartial because I had to be in Milwaukee that evening for a concert and I was concerned that I couldn't properly concentrate on the trial and the evidence in the manner that was required.

"What is the concert?" asked the judge.

"Gordon Lightfoot," I responded.

"OOOHHHH!" said the jury box.

Then the judge excused me from the panel. And while he was being, well, judicious, I also felt that he was being kind, and I can't be sure, but I think I saw just the hint of a smile.

The concert was wonderful. Mr. Lightfoot was in fine voice during the show and jovial afterwards, and I'm very thankful I was able to be there.

Still, I know there may be those who feel that I somehow shirked my civic duty. So if you believe in karma, or penance, or the idea that what goes around comes around, you'll be happy to know that what came around the following Tuesday was a much more difficult case, and I was chosen to be on the jury.

The first thing that happens when you are picked for a jury is that the bailiff confiscates the cellphones (and other contraband) of those who ignored the jury message line. You are then taken to the jury room, your new home away from home for as long as it takes to reach a verdict.

Our trial lasted all day and into the evening. We were frequently sent back to the jury room in between witnesses, where we experienced long silences punctuated by bursts of small talk, which is what happens in a room full of strangers who are forbidden, at that time, from talking about the one thing they really want to discuss.

Jury trials are the only human endeavor I can think of where people go to school for years to learn their craft, apply it as well as they are able, and then, at the most critical point, the entire operation is turned over to a bunch of amateurs.

It would be like the Packers driving down the field and, when they reach the red zone, having Coach McCarthy pull his players in favor of cheesehead-wearing fans picked at random. (And good luck finding enough sober ones.)

We, the amateurs, tried very hard to rise to the occasion. We spent hours discussing evidence and reasonable doubt and points of law that seemed obscure and at times contradictory.

Even with a preponderance of evidence, it is not an easy thing to have a hand in sending another human to prison. And I don't believe we convicted an innocent man, but having experienced the process, I can see how such a thing could happen, even with a jury as diligent and well-intentioned as ours.

In a real trial, mistakes can be made, witnesses can lie, and attorneys don't necessarily display the scripted brilliance of Jack McCoy or his adversaries.

It's not *Law & Order*.

It's life.

Twenty Murdered Children

There are no words.

At least there are none I can think of that would begin to convey the horror and sadness of hopeful, happy first-graders walking (or more likely, skipping) into their classroom on a Friday morning in December, eleven days before Christmas, never to walk out.

But somehow, those of us who remain must find a way to use our words, and our inside voices, in a manner that will honor the memory of those twenty beautiful babies and the six brave women who gave their lives trying to protect the students in their care.

I have stated before, and fervently believe, that had the Founding Fathers been able to gaze across the centuries and envision such things as assault rifles, hollow-point bullets, and an internet where both could be easily purchased, they would have worded the Bill of Rights a little differently.

What we do know is that the Founders were very concerned, and rightfully so, about American citizens having recourse against the sort of tyrannical government from which they had just declared independence.

But when one group—the NRA, for example—behaves as though their particular favorite Constitutional right somehow overrides the need of their fellow citizens to be safe in their schools and workplaces and houses of worship, it becomes its own form of tyranny.

It seems to me that the leadership of the NRA represents the views and interests of the average gun owner about as well as Lance Armstrong represents USA Cycling.

Also, before the Founding Fathers began amending their new document, they stated up front what they hoped to accomplish by writing it in the first place.

To form a more perfect union.

To establish justice.

To promote the general welfare.

Balancing the relationship between individual rights and the needs of the populace—the general welfare—has always been a difficult dance.

After 9/11 and subsequent attempts to sabotage airplanes, much more strict security measures went into effect.

The last time I flew, I had a new bottle of conditioner confiscated. When this happens, we roll our eyes and shake our heads and wonder aloud what the world is coming to.

Then we arrive safely at our destination, buy more conditioner, and get on with our lives.

The relatively minor inconveniences, within reason, are bearable, because travelers not only feel safer; they actually are safer.

There are people I like and respect who feel that background checks on firearms purchases, and limiting certain types of weapons and ammo, are unacceptable infringements upon their rights as law-abiding gun owners.

But I would say that promoting the general welfare suggests otherwise. Waiting a few days to purchase a firearm is at worst an annoyance, and to the best of my knowledge no one has died from it.

A murdered child is a national tragedy, and for the family, a grief from which they will never really recover.

Those same people say that a gun is no more responsible for what the person shooting it does than an automobile is responsible for an accident caused by the person behind the wheel.

And it's true that both are inanimate objects

which, when used unwisely or maliciously, can cause destruction.

But cars were designed as a conveyance. Firearms were designed to shoot projectiles that injure and kill living things.

Yet automobiles are far more regulated. They must be registered, and anyone wishing to drive one has to take classes, pass a proficiency test, and provide proof of insurance.

No one enjoys standing in line at the DMV, but somehow we all manage to survive with our constitutional rights and most of our dignity intact.

Others say our societal sickness isn't due to guns at all, but rather too many violent video games, TV shows, and movies. Yet other countries with which we have much in common—Canada comes to mind—have virtually the same entertainment. Canada has much more stringent gun laws. It also has universal health care, in which people with mental health issues, and their families, may have better access to treatment options. And it has a fraction of the gun violence.

That might not be a coincidence.

The same day as the Sandy Hook massacre, a deranged man in China, armed with a knife, attacked a schoolroom full of children.

It quickly became a Facebook meme—the point being, I guess, that someone who has decided to hurt other people will use whatever weapon they have at their disposal.

And this, of course, is true.

But the meme omitted one rather salient point. In the China attack, not one child died.

Not one.

"Guns don't kill people," came the predictable mantra after Tucson. After Aurora. After Oak Creek. After Kansas City and Portland.

And after Newtown.

As it inevitably will after the next unspeakable tragedy, and the next, and the one after that, until we finally decide we've had enough.

"People kill people."

True enough.

But people with ridiculously easy access to what amounts to weapons of mass destruction are doing an inordinate amount of the killing.

And so it is up to people—of all races, belief systems, and political affiliations—to work together, to have reasonable discussions, and to figure out how to make it stop.

Because it simply has to stop.

Cranium Scrapings

This month's column was going to be called "Jennifer Goes to the Proctologist," in which our heroine prepares for her first-ever colonoscopy, and hilarity (hopefully) ensues.

But then the appointment needed to be rescheduled, and as it seemed premature to write about a procedure before said procedure is—dare I say—behind me, I was left with a looming deadline and a blank legal pad.

And so here, in no particular order of significance, are 600-800 words worth of cranium scrapings to fill those empty pages.

- I have often felt that James Madison and his pals might have worded the first couple of amendments differently had they been able to gaze across the centuries and envision such things as internet porn, assault rifles, and *Citizens United*. But on the topic of religious freedom, a subject with which they were very well acquainted, they got it exactly right. "Congress shall make no law respecting an establishment of religion, or prohibiting the free exercise thereof..." No one should ever be forced to participate in a particular religion—or any religion—and no one should be forbidden from doing so. It's concise, elegant, and profound in its simplicity. I'm not sure why we in the 21st century seem to have such a difficult time grasping what must have seemed so obvious to the Founding Fathers.

- It's very possible that when Robert Frost's character stopped by those woods, he wasn't contemplating his own death. He may simply have thought that the snow looked pretty.

- Numbers don't lie, but people who use them do. Under Scott Walker, Wisconsin gained 30,000 jobs. It also lost 24,000 jobs. 63% of registered voters believe everything they hear in an attack ad. (Okay, I made that last part up.)

- "Divide and Conquer" is a bad strategy, always. Even if it appears to succeed at first, it ultimately fails because what has supposedly been conquered has been diminished in the process.

- When my kids were in school, most of their teachers were good, some were very good, and a few were exceptional. There were a couple of bad ones too, and there needs to be a better system for weeding them out, because a bad teacher, like a bad neurosurgeon (or, for that matter, a bad proctologist) is a dangerous thing. But the vast majority of them were diligent, approachable, and dedicated to the job of helping the students in their care learn and succeed. To paint them as greedy, lazy dilettantes—to imply that "they" are somehow trying to take advantage of "us"—is shameful and toxic and it needs to stop.

- One of life's little pleasures is driving along and, when you activate your turn signal, having the sound of the blinker sync up perfectly with the song you're listening to.

- Every day at work, I talk to people who are trying to find affordable health insurance for themselves and/or their families. Many of them will be unsuccessful, and their stories are heartbreaking. A veteran trying to find coverage for his sick wife. A grieving widow who has been told she is only covered under her late husband's policy for another 30 days. Parents who have suddenly lost their jobs and their insurance and are desperate to make sure that at least their kids will be covered. Meanwhile, members of Congress, and their dependents, are eligible for the Federal Employees Health Benefits Program from the moment they are sworn in. Their coverage begins immediately, and no one gets denied because of a pre-existing condition. On average, 72% of their insurance premiums are paid for by their employer, the federal government —which really means the taxpayers, many of whom are the same people who are trying, and frequently failing, to obtain coverage for themselves and their families.

Obamacare may be flawed, but at least it attempted to address the staggering fact that the United States is the only country in the industrialized world that does not ensure that its citizens have some sort of health care. And if it had been in effect a few years ago, my son would have still been covered under our plan when he broke his wrist, and he would not have had to begin his post-collegiate adult life with $14,000 in medical bills. If it, or part of it, is overturned by the Supreme Court as unconstitutional, which as of this writing seems likely, then the health care debate will begin anew. So if the members of this most hyperpartisan Congress truly want to do something about their historically-low approval rating, and work together to accomplish something good for the people they supposedly represent, this would be an excellent place to start.

- Aging is inevitable; getting old is a choice.

- Common sense isn't.

One of the Big Kids

When I was young, voting seemed like one of the very grown-up activities that defined adulthood.

Or perhaps I should say that it was one of the adult-defining activities that children were permitted to watch.

I remember going to the polling place with my mother and looking at all the grown-up legs and feet sticking out from underneath the curtain that surrounded the voting booth. It was very exciting, because to a child, anything that happens behind a curtain is inherently fascinating.

When it was our turn, my mother pulled a lever which closed the curtain around us. It was not as fascinating as it had seemed from the outside, perhaps because I was too short to see what was happening. Still, it was pretty cool just to be included in something so mysteriously adult.

When my mother had made her selections, she pushed the lever back to its original position, which simultaneously registered her votes, opened the curtain, rang a little bell, and caused the entire structure to shake.

Now THAT'S voting.

When I voted recently, I went to the same elementary school my children attended, where I waited in line to get my voting sheet, took it to a little plastic half-desk, and colored in the little ovals next to my candidates' names with a special pencil that was tethered to the desk with string.

It might still be the same solemn civic responsibility my parents engaged in, but it felt more like filling out a first-grade worksheet—especially since, when I was finished, I got a sticker.

(Speaking of first grade, I'm not going to waste any of my allotted words drawing obvious comparisons between childishness and the most recent onslaught of campaign attack ads. But if you are playing along at home and you want to go there, it's all right with me. I won't be offended.)

Voting is just one example of how a milestone in life, upon arrival, can look and feel very different than you thought it would when you were striving so hard to get there.

This disparity between perception and reality was beautifully articulated more than forty years ago by noted philosopher (and my grade-school classmate) Shirley Yzenbaard, who observed:

"When we were little, we thought the sixth-graders were so big and so cool. But now WE'RE the sixth-graders, and we're the same dumb kids we've always been!"

More recently, I have been gleaning wisdom from another noted philosopher: my cocker spaniel, Dexter.

Dexter is a senior citizen now, and lately he has been dealing with health issues. Some are self-inflicted (soreness from lewd and lascivious behavior at the dog park and with his much-younger doggie cousin), but most are because of advancing age and a degenerative arthritic condition in his back.

It was so bad a few months ago that we had begun to fear that the day every pet owner dreads might be imminent. But thankfully, rest and different medications have Dexter acting like his old self again.

But his old self is now, well, old. He's slowing down. He doesn't hear as well. He can't really jump any more.

But Dexter is not one to dwell upon what he is no longer able to do. Not being able to jump gave him the opportunity to learn a new trick, and now he uses Doggy Steps to access his favorite spot on the couch.

On our walks, he stops to smell not just the roses, but seemingly, each individual blade of grass.

He stops and lifts his muzzle to the breeze, letting it play with his ears and ruffle his fur and bring him even more wonderful scents.

These days it takes us as long to get around the block as it used to take us to walk a mile. But Dexter knows, and I am learning, that it isn't just about the destination or how quickly we can get there.

It's about enjoying the journey, and being grateful that there's still a journey to enjoy.

I have come to believe that, as we age, we display more of who we really are.

We grow into ourselves.

And if we're paying attention, we can learn things.

One of the main things I have learned so far is how much I don't know. I still have a lot to learn.

I think this is a good thing, because it allows me to keep asking questions. It could even be a sign of maturity.

Of course, it could also be the onset of dementia, but I'm trying to stay positive.

If the calendar is to be believed, I have now been on this planet for more than half a century.

Yet I am, essentially, the same dumb kid I've always been.

They say admitting it is the first step.

Bread and Family Circuses

The freshest bread at the store is always hanging out at the back of the shelf, and so I was working my way, as carefully and surreptitiously as possible, through the Brownberry™ Oatnut when I heard a voice behind me.

"There sure is a lot of bread, isn't there?"

I turned around, expecting to see a mildly-disgruntled store employee, but there was no one there except a pleasant-looking gentleman who, as it turned out, was extremely eager to talk about bread.

So, for the next several minutes, we (and by "we" I mean "he") had a discussion about all the various types of bread at our neighborhood grocery store.

We finally said our goodbyes, and I was headed for the relative solitude of the canned-vegetable aisle when my bread buddy approached me again, because he needed to tell me of a show he had seen on the History Channel about how the Egyptians invented batteries.

This sort of thing happens to me frequently enough that I have begun to suspect that it may not be mere coincidence.

Also, it appears to be genetic.

On a recent Wednesday, my son Andrew and I had made plans to meet at the dog park so that my dog Dexter could run around with Andrew's dog Sampson (who happens to be the cutest, smartest, most adorable grandpuppy EVER). Wednesday is Andrew's day off, and since it was the day before my birthday, I asked him if I could have a little of his time.

"You can have a ton of my time," he said.

But rain thwarted our dog park plans, so we decided to go looking at car dealerships for the particular Subaru that Andrew has been trying to find.

And that's how we happened to meet Ken, whose occupation is car sales but whose passion, we would soon learn, resides elsewhere.

Ken began by asking Andrew what make and model he was looking for, the color, the name of Andrew's girlfriend, whether he had played football—in short, all the usual questions you ask of someone seeking a Subaru. And somehow, the subject came up of Andrew's long-ago snowboarding accident.

My son comes from a long line of oddly-kneed Perry men, but the accident, which snapped his femur and tore a quad tendon, among other things, turned his left knee into something rather exquisitely grotesque.

When your knee can do things that make an actual doctor say, "Dude, cut that out!" you know you've got something.

So naturally, Ken wanted to see it.

And it was while Andrew was rolling up his pant leg that I spotted the picture on Ken's desk of someone who looked much like Ken, except with a black pompadour, huge sideburns, and wearing a white jumpsuit.

For Ken, you see, is an Elvis enthusiast. At least that's the term my son Matt suggested, as "Elvis Impersonator" is apparently passé and possibly derogatory.

Ken began to regale us with stories of past trips to Graceland, and told us of how he manages someone in an event called "The King of the World," which we gathered to be some sort of competition among the Elvii. (I suppose it could also involve a large ship and Celine Dion, but I digress. My story will go on.)

It may well be that I am so fond of these memorable little encounters because it is becoming increasingly likely that I will be the initiator of them.

Last December, on a late Sunday afternoon that would have been described as dark and gloomy except that the Packers had won that day, I went shopping with Andrew and his girlfriend—whose name, as Ken could tell you, is Becky—to get Andrew a winter coat as a Christmas present.

Leaving the store, I was walking briskly and got to Andrew's car first. I got into the front passenger seat, buckled in, and then noticed the word "Focus" on the glove compartment.

"Focus?" I thought. "But Andrew drives a Jetta... OH, CRAP!!!"

I jumped out, hoping that my two young companions hadn't seen anything.

But judging by their doubled-over postures, it was pretty clear that they had.

They had been watching—Becky in horror, Andrew in what could best be described as gleeful anticipation—as I approached the similar, but clearly not identical vehicle. They had seen everything.

Once I was safely belted into the Jetta, Andrew turned to me. "We must not speak of this again," he said.

Which meant, of course, that he would speak of it to everyone he could, as soon as possible.

Who doesn't lock their car doors in a busy parking lot? Because, really, you should.

Otherwise you're liable to find a confused old woman sitting in the passenger seat, waiting to go home.

And on the way, she's probably going to talk about bread.

After the Attack

Having finished showering, I opened the bathroom door, and almost immediately the hallway smoke detector began to beep.

I have set off our smoke alarm many times—"Dinner's ready!" my son Andrew would shout—but never by simply opening the bathroom door, and it was a little unsettling.

Our dog Dexter was a year old, just a puppy, and we had only had him for a few months, so we were still under the mistaken impression that he was a normal dog. Barking at the smoke alarm seemed like a perfectly reasonable response.

He and I checked the house to make sure that nothing was on fire, and then I continued getting ready for work.

Back then I worked at a bookstore in Oshkosh, and I was looking forward to the drive down in my little red Dodge Neon, especially on that beautiful September morning.

It was a little after 8:00 A.M. CDT, and since the Neon had no CD player I was listening to the radio. I caught the end of a news update that mentioned a plane crash in New York. By the time I reached the highway, there had been another update about another plane crash.

"They must have really bad air traffic control," said the DJ, prompting me to switch to a news station.

By the time I arrived in Oshkosh, the world was upside down.

Someone at the store found a radio, and we listened in shock as the Twin Towers fell.

I drove home in a fog, wanting nothing more than to hug my children when they came home from school.

Andrew went off to be with a friend. Matt, who was a junior in high school, told me that he needed to do some homework for his Environmental Science class that involved going to the habitat he had chosen, the woods at the Thousand Islands Nature Center.

Looking back, I doubt that he needed to do homework as much as he needed the peacefulness and solitude of the woods.

He had his license, but no car, and he didn't drive the Neon with its manual transmission, so we went together.

I walked through the silent woods and looked up into the flawless sky, trying, unsuccessfully, to comprehend the horror unfolding a thousand miles to the east.

Back at home, I realized that I had some ground beef that needed to be used. I didn't know what to do about that. When your country has been attacked, is it all right to go ahead and make tacos?

We watched the news, wanting to learn as much as we could about what had happened. We watched interviews with people who were holding handmade signs, trying frantically to locate their missing loved ones. We watched the footage of people running from the clouds of smoke and ash. And we watched, over and over and over again, the planes flying into the towers.

Nine days earlier, we had gone down to my in-laws' house for an early Labor Day cookout. Driving home that evening, I turned on the radio to listen to the Sunday night baseball game.

The Red Sox were playing the Yankees. We came into the game around the sixth inning, and it soon became apparent that this was no ordinary affair, because the Yankees' Mike Mussina was pitching a perfect game.

Every Red Sox out elicited cheers that came

blasting out of the radio. You could hear the tension and excitement in the announcers' voices.

With two outs in the ninth, Red Sox pinch hitter Carl Everett hit a solid single to left. The crowd groaned, and then gave Mussina a long and well-deserved ovation.

But here's the really interesting part—the game was being played in Boston.

That would be exactly like a cheese-wearing crowd at Lambeau Field cheering wildly...for the Minnesota Vikings.

That night the fans in Boston understood, as most of us can when we choose to, that there are things bigger than ourselves, stronger than a rivalry, more important than the things that divide us.

Back in September 2001, we vowed to never forget. And we haven't, but we have become distracted—by wars and recession, by bailouts and the doomsday chalkboards of cable news personalities, by partisan meanness and endless arguments over climate change and immigration and exactly how far from Ground Zero a mosque ought to be.

In these days, it can be hard to remember that in the aftermath of 9/11, something amazing happened: people were nice to each other.

Everyone understood that everyone else was wounded, and so in the weeks following the attacks, people were a little more patient, a little more thoughtful, a little more willing to help each other out.

It would be nice to live in a world where treating each other with kindness and compassion is not merely a temporary reaction to a national tragedy, but a way of life.

That would truly show respect for the victims, and the heroes, of 9/11. Honoring the fallen and caring for the living are both acts of patriotism.

If we remember nothing else, it would be good to remember that.

RED HOT (flash) FANTASY

My boss—we'll call him "Chuck"—is friendly, cheerful, and generous of spirit.

He may also be evil incarnate.

There's just no other way to explain how he so easily enticed me to do that which I swore I would never do—join a fantasy football league.

"C'mon!" he said. "It'll be fun!" (Later he explained that what he meant was, "It'll be fun for the rest of us to watch you!")

And it was fun...at first. This league was just for the playoffs, and each team owner chose one, and only one, player from each of the twelve playoff teams.

I enjoyed putting my team together. My hardest decision ended up being a choice between the Arizona Cardinals' two Pro Bowl wideouts, Larry Fitzgerald and Anquan Boldin. After much vacillating, I went, to my eternal regret, with Boldin. (During the season he was nearly beheaded and only missed a few games; I felt I could count on him.)

On the first Saturday of the playoffs, my dog Dexter and I were on the couch watching the Cardinals host the Atlanta Falcons in the first wildcard game. And it was then that I discovered that what I feared would happen by being a fantasy team owner is exactly what did happen: it completely changed the way I watched the games.

So when Kurt Warner threw a beautiful spiral to Fitzgerald for a touchdown, instead of appreciating the acrobatic endzone catch, I was jumping off the couch and screaming, "Don't throw it to him! Throw it to Boldin!"

Which upset the dog.

Boldin did eventually catch a touchdown pass of his own, and then left the game with a hamstring injury.

Which upset me.

And young Mr. Fitzgerald continued to gobble up every pass in his vicinity like a dreadlocked Pac-Man™.

Which I don't want to talk about any more.

The next day Dexter and I were back on the couch to watch my Philadelphia Eagle, Brian Westbrook, take on the hated Vikings. Westbrook was having a quiet game until finally breaking off a long touchdown run.

Which got me off the couch and screaming again, but in a good way.

Except that it startled my son Matt, who had come over for dinner and isn't really used to seeing his mother behave like that.

It wouldn't have been so bad, but I fear that Matt has already started to think that I'm becoming a bit unhinged.

One day he had come over when it was particularly cold, and noticed me shivering.

"Are you cold?" he asked.

I nodded, pleased with his sensitivity.

Then he said: "Can't you just have a hot flash?"

(It seems that despite all my precautions, Matt has discovered my secret identity: I am Hormone Girl, and shooting heat rays out of my pores is my superpower.)

But I haven't yet mastered my abilities, which is why I have been intrigued all winter with those ubiquitous commercials for the blanket with sleeves.

Clearly, it has the power to change my life.

I know this because the commercial shows

a woman sitting on a couch, uncomfortably wrapped in a traditional blanket. Apparently the phone is ringing, but the woman isn't answering it—she is looking at it distastefully, as though it had just said something obscene or emitted a terrible odor.

But then the same woman is shown wearing the blanket with sleeves, and all is well. She and the phone have reconciled, and in fact seem very happy together.

Other people are shown watching TV, eating popcorn, roasting marshmallows, and even cheering in the bleachers at an unspecified athletic event attended by eight people. Admittedly, they do look a little like cult members, albeit toasty warm ones.

BUT WAIT! If I call RIGHT NOW, they'll send me TWO!

Unfortunately, Matt has vowed never to come over again if he ever finds me wearing even one. It would be a sign to him that I've gone completely over the edge.

So I must try to say no to the blanket with sleeves, and rely solely on Dexter to keep me warm and protect me from my phone.

Except that lately Dexter has been acting a little strange. There could be many reasons for this, but I blame the negative influence of Toy, Dexter's favorite toy.

Toy is a stick covered with tennis-ball fuzz that Dexter picked out himself on a trip to the pet store, and the two of them are nearly inseparable. But recently I've been finding Toy all over the house, and usually in a spot where someone, most likely me, is liable to trip over him.

Toy is a bad seed.

Still, I'm sure there's a perfectly reasonable explanation for why I always seem to find him right outside the bedroom door in the middle of the night.

I certainly don't think that it's because my beloved dog, and his beloved toy, are conspiring to do me harm.

And even if I did think that, *which I don't*, I wouldn't say anything, because that, as Matt likes to remind me, is the sort of talk that makes people institutionalize their parents.

So I will try very hard to remain silent, but if I just can't help myself, I hope that you will feel free to visit me at whatever facility Matt ends up choosing.

I'll be the one in the red blanket, frantically trying to free my arms, screaming at Kurt Warner.

The Reports of My Twittering Have Been Greatly Exaggerated

You never know where you'll be when you find out that you have died.

In February 2010, during the Olympics, Gordon Lightfoot was driving to his office in Toronto when he heard on the radio that he had passed away.

This came as a bit of a surprise, though he did say later that it explained why they were suddenly playing so much of his music.

As so often happens these days, the (thankfully) false rumor turned out to be a case of Twittering gone awry. It's one of the negative aspects of living in a time where anything that happens anywhere gets reported worldwide within moments of its occurrence—or non-occurrence, as the case may be.

I have not yet had to deal with my own demise, but I have experienced an inadvertent slide off the grid.

We had decided to switch our phone service to the digital package offered by our cable provider. This, we thought in an ignorance-is-bliss kind of way, had proceeded without incident, and we were loving the phone service and the features that came with it.

Caller ID is one thing, but caller ID on the TV is something else, and I never tire of it, because apparently I am easily amused.

Looking back, I should have suspected that something was amiss when, a few weeks after the switch, I began receiving cheery "Welcome to the Neighborhood!" packets addressed to someone whose name is similar, but not identical, to mine.

But life went on until I found out that someone who needed to get in touch with me had tried to get my number from directory assistance, and was told that they couldn't have it because my number is unlisted.

This had not been our intention, so I called our cable/phone provider. After fifteen minutes on hold, the young man who took my call looked up my information and then uttered this memorable line:

"You're not listed as unlisted."

I pondered that. "So," I ventured finally, "I'm listed as listed?"

"That's correct. You're listed as listed."

"Then why am I unlisted?"

He put me back on hold for another fifteen minutes.

We think the problem occurred when the information was transferred from the cable company to the phone directory.

To my phone and cable provider, I am me, and I am listed.

In the telephone directory, I am listed, but I am not myself.

So if you need to reach me and you don't have my number, you should probably just send me a message on Facebook.

Facebook, which I enjoy, Twitter, which I find ridiculous, and digital and cellular phones are all forms of communication that were unimaginable a few decades ago. (For me they were unimaginable a few years ago, when I didn't even know how to reply to an email.)

But here they are. And not everyone believes that's a good thing.

In his book *Eating the Dinosaur*, Chuck Klosterman writes that "The benefits of technology are easy to point out...but they do not compensate for the overall loss of humanity that is its inevitable consequence. As a species, we have never been less human than we are right now."

I agree with that. I also disagree.

It's true that time spent Facebooking, Twittering, and World of Warcrafting is time not being spent interacting with actual flesh-and-blood humans at the coffee shop, the dog park, or over the backyard fence. Modern social networking can create a faux intimacy that may hinder or even destroy relationships in the real world.

If you let it.

I believe that ultimately, the experience of being human comes down to what it always has—the choices we make and the ramifications of those choices.

And it's also true that technology gives us opportunities to enrich our lives in wonderful and completely unexpected ways.

As an example, I wrote an article a few years ago about my fondness for the aforementioned Mr. Lightfoot. It was discovered online by a woman named Char who has been living a life in Ontario that has in many ways been almost eerily similar to mine. We began corresponding, and she has become a good friend in the real world as well as the virtual one.

A few years ago, it never would have happened.

That same humble little article found its way to the office of Gordon Lightfoot himself, the same one to which he was headed when he learned that he had died.

And because of that, on March 30, 2008, at the Performing Arts Center in Appleton, Wisconsin, I had the sublime and surreal experience of hearing Gordon Lightfoot tell the packed house how much he had appreciated my article. Or, as my son Matt said to my husband, "Gordon called Mom out!"

There's really no way to describe what that was

like, except to say that it's all the affirmation I should need for the next hundred years or so.

And by then, death probably will have found me, even if I am unlisted.

Knots and Loose Ends

As the mother of the groom at a destination wedding, my biggest responsibility was deciding whether to wear sandals or go barefoot.

The choice was made when a pair of multi-colored wedges coyly beckoned to me from the sale rack at Kohl's. I had no way of knowing at the time that they were flesh-gouging monsters cleverly disguised in an adorable size 7 ½ package. In that moment, I only knew that they perfectly matched the little blue sheath that had whispered my name a few minutes earlier.

With my footwear conundrum resolved, I was free to devote all my time and energy to dreading the flight to the Dominican Republic.

As I have grown older, I have begun to realize more and more the importance of not focusing solely on the destination, but on enjoying and appreciating the journey.

Clearly, however, this is in a metaphorical sense.

In the real world, for me at least, it's much easier to enjoy the journey when the journey does not involve air travel.

Obviously, I would have found a way to travel anywhere for the wedding, because I love my kids more than I hate to fly.

But I *really* hate to fly.

Andrew and Becky were aware of this, and it was a factor in their choice of Punta Cana, a vacation paradise on the eastern end of the Dominican Republic and a relatively manageable 4 ½ hour flight from Chicago.

(Of O'Hare International Airport—ORD, to your luggage—I will not speak. I don't want to waste any of my allotted words, and besides, many of those words would be unprintable.)

The only enjoyable part of flying for me is the sense of euphoria I feel when the plane's wheels touch the runway. And in this case it definitely didn't hurt that we gained 45 degrees and proximity to the beach.

On one of my first beach walks, I was approached—accosted might be a better word—by an older gentleman in a Speedo, a species I normally try to avoid.

"Boston?" he asked in an accent I couldn't quite place.

This was the week after the Marathon, and I figured he had chosen a random, harmless-looking American with whom to discuss the bombing, or perhaps express his condolences.

"I'm not from Boston," I told him. "But I've been there. It's a beautiful city."

"Unacceptable!" He was almost yelling, which seemed odd.

Unsure what to do next, I offered, "But I cheered for them when they won the World Series."

He shook his head. "Not a fan!" He started to walk away, but then turned back, apparently to give me one last chance.

"Boston...Public...Library?"

I shook my head, and he shuffled away.

Some things are just not meant to be. Or, at least to be understood. At all.

This sort of thing seems to happen to our family a lot, and happily, Becky has shown every sign of being able to take it in stride.

The weather in Punta Cana was flawless...except for the day of the wedding. The skies opened up on Becky and her mom as they were returning from the salon where Becky had gotten her hair and makeup done a few hours before the ceremony.

Her wedding dress, and Andrew's clothes, were several hours late in arriving. The night before, one of Andrew's wedding flip-flops had become lodged in a tree during a well-intentioned but ultimately futile attempt to liberate a coconut. Through it all, Becky remained calm.

And somehow, at 5 PM on April 27, everything was perfect.

Watching a beloved child-turned-adult get married is wonderful and poignant in a way that is difficult to put into words.

I will never forget how lovely Becky looked as she walked down the aisle, or Andrew's expression as he turned and saw her for the first time.

Amazingly, the photographer managed to capture all of it, even though I don't even remember him being there.

After we got back, we had dinner with our friends Bruce and Jean, who have known Andrew his entire life.

Looking at the wedding album, Jean remarked how nice it would be if I could travel back in time and show the pictures to kindergarten Andrew, and tell him, "See? This is how it's all going to turn out."

I'm not sure kindergarten Andrew would have been able to comprehend what he was seeing, just as, at that time, he wasn't able to put words on a difficult year with a teacher who had very little compassion or patience for squirmy five-year-old boys.

But it certainly would have been a great comfort to kindergarten Andrew's mother.

The things we deal with as parents—tantrums, bad report cards, puberty, all of it—would be so much easier to endure if we could just somehow be assured that, eventually, everything turns out all right.

That after all the challenges, and the second-guessing, and the mistakes, there will come a time when you will see your son living his life with confidence and joy, knowing he will be returning from his wedding with his beautiful bride to their house, and their dog, and a job that he loves.

That one day you will be able to sit on the beach and gaze up into the night sky and breathe a sigh at the wonder of it all, and the ocean breeze will carry the unformed words away, almost like a prayer...

Thank you.

Made in the USA
Lexington, KY
11 March 2014